Rice

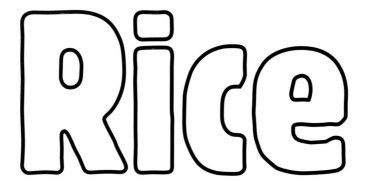

Roz Denny

First published in Great Britain by Heinemann Library
Halley Court, Jordan Hill, Oxford OX2 8EJ,
a division of Reed Educational and Professional Publishing Ltd.

Heinemann is a registered trademark of Reed Educational and
Professional Publishing Ltd.

OXFORD FLORENCE PRAGUE MADRID ATHENS
MELBOURNE AUCKLAND KUALA LUMPUR SINGAPORE TOKYO
IBADAN NAIROBI KAMPALA JOHANNESBURG GABORONE
PORTSMOUTH NH (USA) CHICAGO MEXICO CITY SAO PAULO

Designed by Celia Floyd
Illustrations by Barry Atkinson, pp. 10, 11, 13, 20, 21, 23, 26, 28;
Oxford Illustrators, pp. 6, 8
Printed in Hong Kong / China

02 01 00 99 98
10 9 8 7 6 5 4 3 2 1

ISBN 0 431 08874 8

British Library Cataloguing in Publication Data

Denny, Roz
  Rice. - (Food in focus)
  1.Rice - Juvenile literature
  I.Title
  664.7'25

Acknowledgements

The Publishers would like to thank the following for permission to reproduce
photographs:

Anthony Blake Photo Library, p. 17 (W. Double), p. 24 (Rosenfield), p. 12 (John Sims);
Gareth Boden, pp. 13, 18, 25, 27, 29; Hulton Getty, p. 7; Oxford Scientific Films, p. 19
(P & W. Ward); Tilda, p. 16; Tony Stone, p. 14 (Chris Everad), p. 20 (Gray Mortimore);
Trip, pp. 9 (top), 14 (C.C), p. 4 (W. Jacobs); Zefa, pp. 9 (bottom), 10, p. 5 (Lombardi).

Cover photograph: Trevor Clifford

Contents

Introduction   4

The history of rice   6

Where does rice grow?   8

How is rice cultivated?   10

Refining rice   12

Rice in Asia   14

Rice in the Middle East and Europe   16

Rice in the New World   18

Rice and health   20

Experiments with rice   22

How to cook rice   24

Rice pilaff   26

Rice salad   28

Glossary   30

Further reading   31

Index   32

Some words are shown in bold, **like this**. You can find out what they mean by looking in the Glossary.

Introduction

Rice is the staple food for over half the world's population, many of whom eat it with every meal. It was one of the first **cereals** to be **cultivated**, although exactly how long ago is not clear. Growing rice requires great skill and a lot of labour, so rice farmers must work well together to ensure good harvests. Consequently, over the centuries many cultural and religious practices have developed around the cultivation of rice.

Most rice is eaten throughout Asia, from India to Japan. But rice dishes are also very popular in the Middle East, Mediterranean countries, Africa, parts of the United States of America and the West Indies. In many other countries where wheat is the main cereal food, such as northern Europe, rice is eaten only occasionally, often as a dessert. However, as more people from northern countries become aware of the delicious **cuisine** of rice-eating nations, the demand for different rices is increasing.

Children in the Far East eat rice several times a day

Rice grains are affected by climate, soil and growing conditions, so as the cultivation of rice spread over the centuries, many different varieties developed. There are now around 85,000 varieties of rice throughout the world – all suitable for different uses, both in factories and in the home. A variety that may cook well in a domestic kitchen and be light, with nice separate grains, may not do as well when prepared in a large factory cooker.

There are many different varieties of rice

There are also many other ways in which rice can be used. In China, Japan and South East Asia rice is ground and used to make a form of light pasta which is then cut into noodles. Rice can be used to make wines and vinegars; coarse-grain ground rice, finer flour and rice paper for baking; crisp crackers (rice cakes) for snacks and – of course – puffed into the famous rice breakfast cereals that snap, crackle and pop!

Rice is a healthy food – it gives our bodies lots of energy. It is easy to store, cooks easily and – most important of all – is quite cheap and filling. Rice is very digestible and the goodness from it can be absorbed into our bodies quickly, which makes it ideal to feed to babies and sick people who find it hard to eat very much. It is also very versatile and there are a great many delicious dishes that can be made with rice – sweet or savoury, hot or cold.

The history of rice

Historians find it hard to put an exact date on when rice was first grown. In many parts of the ancient world it gradually replaced millet and other **cereals** because early farmers found they got bigger and better crops with rice.

The migration of rice

There is evidence that rice was first **cultivated** from wild grains about 5000 years ago, in northern India, and then spread eastward to South East Asia, China and Japan, and westward to the Middle East and Persia (now Iran). The ancient Greeks and Romans knew about rice, but regarded it as an exotic medicine. However, modern Greeks and Italians are now great eaters of rice and have a number of their own national rice dishes.

When the Moors from Arabia conquered Spain in the early Middle Ages they started rice cultivation. Many Spanish dishes now use rice. From Spain, rice was taken westward to Portugal and eastward to the south of France and the Po Valley in northern Italy. Rice soon became an important crop in these European countries although the type of grain grown was a rounder grain. In Italy this rice has developed into **risotto** grains which give a light creaminess to dishes when cooked.

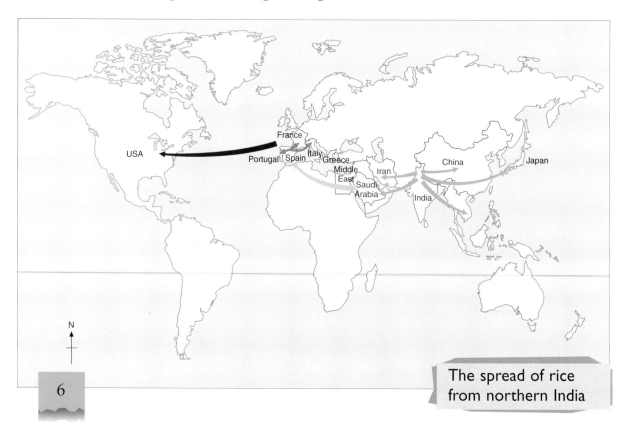

The spread of rice from northern India

Thomas Jefferson, the third president of the United States of America

Thomas Jefferson – the rice missionary

By the late seventeenth and eighteenth centuries rice introduced by early European settlers was grown in Carolina in North America and exported to Europe. One of America's famous historical figures, Thomas Jefferson – eventually to become president of the new United States of America – was a very keen gardener and botanist with an interest in agriculture, particularly the growing of rice. Many of Jefferson's friends would send back samples of rice seed from their travels abroad for him to plant and experiment with.

Before he became president, Jefferson was made the United States of America's first ambassador to Paris. While he was in Europe he decided to visit Italy to find out more about rice-growing. At that time it was illegal to take unrefined rice from one country to another, so he smuggled rice grains out of Italy in his pockets to take back to Carolina. Even today, many cooks still refer to 'Carolina' rice in recipes although little rice is grown there now.

Where does rice grow?

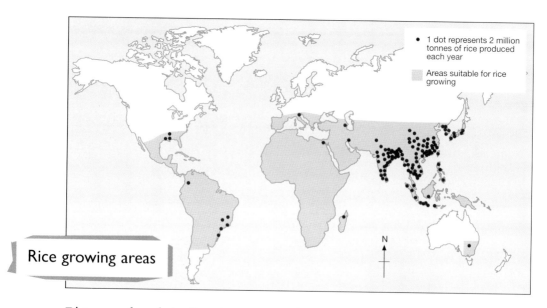

- 1 dot represents 2 million tonnes of rice produced each year

Areas suitable for rice growing

N

Rice growing areas

Rice needs a lot of water at certain stages of its growth. The supply of water is maintained by **irrigation**, through hand-dug ditches and barriers. This affects the look of the landscape.

Countries with the right conditions for rice-growing form a wide band across the world – from Spain and the southern states of the United States of America in the northern hemisphere, down to the tip of South Africa in the southern hemisphere. Rice is a very adaptable plant and as growing conditions can vary widely within this part of the world, strains of rice have been developed that can withstand lower temperatures or grow with less water.

In very fertile and well-irrigated areas, rice farmers aim to grow two or even three crops a year. Certain top-quality varieties, which rely solely on rain for water, may only be harvested once a year and so they are more expensive.

The beauty of rice terraces

Rice can only be grown on flat ground so in countries where the countryside is hilly, **paddy fields** have been built out of the hillside as level **terraces**. This can make the landscape look quite beautiful and many of the terraces are hundreds of years old. Terraces can be found in the Philippines, Indonesia, Thailand and China. Perhaps the most famous rice terraces, reputed to be over 2000 years old, are in the Philippines in an area called Banaue.

Farmers make flat terraces on the hills for long, thin paddy fields

Looking for a Green Revolution

The Philippines is the home of the International Rice Research Institute (IRRI) where scientists carry out valuable work developing new super-breeds of rice to feed the rapidly increasing population in Asia. Growing enough rice to feed the extra millions of people is very important for governments and agricultural scientists.

Modern rice landscapes

Where rice farming is mechanized, paddy fields tend to be larger. In the United States of America, in the southern states of Arkansas, Texas, Louisiana and around the Mississippi Delta, the paddy fields are very large and the rice is grown mostly for export and industrial uses. As a result, the USA is now the world's second largest exporter of rice. Thailand is the largest.

Large, flat paddy fields are used in modern rice growing

How is rice cultivated?

The botanical name of the rice plant is *Oryza sativa*. There are two sub-divisions of the **species** – long grain rice and short grain rice. The rice plant can grow in a wide range of climates and in a great number of varieties, reaching heights of 1–6 metres. In general all the varieties look the same. The stalk is hollow so it can soak up moisture from the roots which are planted in water. At the top of the plant are the **panicles**, each with clusters of **spikelets** with the actual rice grains inside.

Unrefined rice grains are known as **paddy**. Only when the grains are harvested and outer husks removed is it called rice. That is why farmers use the term 'paddy fields' to describe where they grow rice.

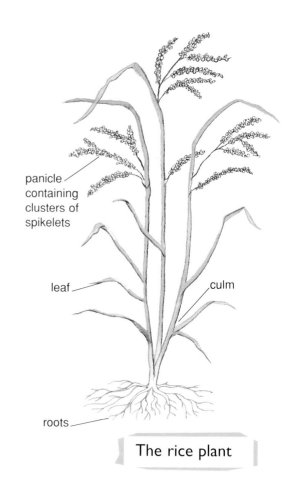

panicle containing clusters of spikelets

leaf

culm

roots

The rice plant

Rice-growing in traditional areas

In most parts of Asia, seeds are first sprouted in seed beds. The tiny seedlings are then re-planted in flooded fields so they have more space to grow. In Asian countries this is done by hand, mostly by women who spend all their time ankle-deep in muddy water. Flooding the fields also stop weeds from growing.

One of the side benefits of flooded fields is that wild-life such as frogs, birds, insects and even fish can grow in and around the water. Their waste products can fertilize the crop as manure.

When the paddy ripens, the flooded fields are drained and the plants are harvested by hand. Bundles of stalks are beaten to shake off the whole grains, which are then dried in the sun. After that the paddy rice is crushed to get the grains out of the husks and then **winnowed** (tossed in the air), so that the loose husks blow away.

Modern rice-growing

In America, and certain parts of Australia, rice is produced by modern mechanized methods. This cuts down on the back-breaking hard work of the more traditional rice-growing methods used in most parts of Asia. There are many rice-growing regions in America, from California to Texas and the Mississippi Delta. These grow a wide range of varieties from Japanese-style short grain rices to long grain rices that imitate Indian rices. Seeds are sown onto very large fields from aeroplanes. When ripe, the plants are harvested and separated into straw and grain by giant combine-harvesters.

Planting rice seedlings by hand is very hard work

What's in a grain of rice?

The centre part, where the starch is stored, is called the endosperm. This is covered by the outer bran layers and finally the husk or glume. At the base of the endosperm is the small embryo or germ. If you hold a single grain of white rice in your hand you can clearly see the denser embryo at the base.

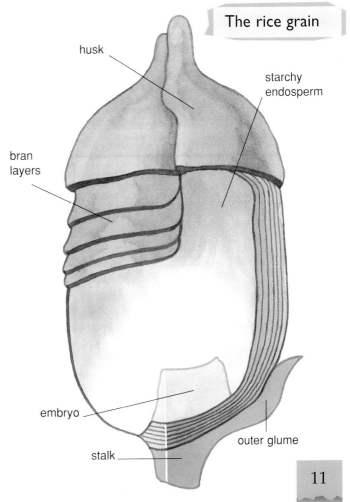

The rice grain

husk

starchy endosperm

bran layers

embryo

stalk

outer glume

11

Refining rice

In Asian countries almost all rice grown is eaten by the local people. To extract the edible grain, the **paddy** grains are either refined by traditional methods, or collected by companies and milled in modern and computerized factories. Farmers in Asia who sell their crops to these companies take it to rice markets where buyers from the large companies choose the best quality grains. These are sent on to rice refineries where the paddy is stored in silos.

Farmers bring their rice crops to sell at this market

At the beginning of the refining process the paddy must be cleaned, first in a machine called a scalper and then by air. Any small stones collected with the paddy are also removed by machine.

At this stage the paddy is still quite moist, which reduces its storage life, so the paddy is passed through large driers several times until it has the right low moisture content.

When it is time for the outside husk to be removed, the grains are fed between two rubber rollers. These run at different speeds, which causes the husk to come off. Now the paddy becomes real rice!

For brown rice, the outer bran layers are left intact. For white rice the bran layer is removed, either by rubbing each grain against a rough surface, or by rubbing the grains together.

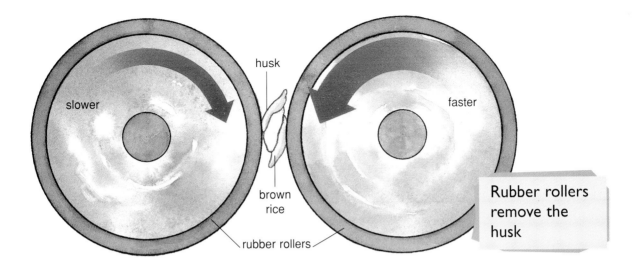

husk

slower

faster

brown rice

rubber rollers

Rubber rollers remove the husk

Parboiled rice

Rice can also undergo a high pressure steaming process to seal the outside of the grain. This is called the gelatinization of starch. It is based on an ancient Persian method of heat-treating rice grains so they could be stored for longer. It also helps the rice grains to stay separate during cooking and keeps in more vitamins, but it can affect the natural aromatic flavour and slightly increases the cooking time. This kind of rice is sold as 'easycook' or 'parboiled' rice.

The nutritious outer bran layer is removed from brown rice to produce white rice

White rice or brown?

Most Asian people like white, or polished, rice. For this kind of rice, the outer bran layer is removed and the grains are dried and rolled. This makes the rice quicker to cook and more delicate in flavour. However, the outer bran layer is very nutritious as it contains valuable vitamins and dietary fibre. If a person eats only polished white rice without the bran layer and very little else, as happened in prisoner-of-war camps during World War II, life-threatening illnesses such as beri-beri can develop. In the United States of America, rice must be enriched with extra vitamins, by law.

Rice in Asia

Both long and short grain rices are found in Asian countries. Usually, long grain rices cook into separate fluffy grains whilst short grain rices are either creamy or sticky. However, there are also crossovers, such as long grain Thai rices, that become slightly sticky when cooked.

Most of the time rice is cooked 'plain boiled' for everyday meals. In Japan, parts of China and South East Asia, people like their rice sticky. Sticky rice is easier to eat with chop sticks. It is considered quite polite to hold the rice bowl up to your face and push rice into your mouth.

Sushi style

The Japanese like to eat cold, sticky rice wrapped in seaweed. This is called **sushi**. *Sushi*-making is regarded by the Japanese as a great art and it takes several years for a *sushi* chef to train.

Once the rice is cooked it is dressed with rice vinegar, sugar and salt, then cooled quickly with fans. Sheets of paper-thin seaweed are laid out and spread with the sticky rice. Coloured foods such as omelette strips, cucumber sticks, fish eggs or raw fish can be added. The seaweed is then rolled up in bamboo mats and cut in slices. *Sushi* can also be made by rolling rice into balls and enclosing them with very fresh raw fish.

In China

Many people in China eat **congee**, a savoury rice 'soup', for breakfast. They also like to fry cooked rice with soy sauce, egg shreds and tasty vegetables. One favourite Chinese dessert is called 'Eight treasures rice' which is a rich, creamy, sweet rice decorated with fruits.

The Japanese make delicious snacks with cold rice, called sushi

In India

People in India eat many types of rice dishes such as **pilaus** or *dhosas* (rice pancakes) although much of the time rice is served 'plain boiled'. The best quality Indian rice is **basmati**, grown at the foothills of the Himalayas in the area known as Haryana. It is also called 'the prince of rices' because it has a long, elegant grain with a beautiful natural aroma. In fact *basmati* means 'fragrance' in Hindi.

> ### *Did you know?*
>
> - *In Thailand, rice is considered to be the link between heaven and earth. Both the king of Thailand and the emperor of Japan are involved in religious ceremonies involving the planting of rice.*

In many parts of South East Asia, rice is stored in specially carved barns, which local people believe are holy places. Rice spirits are worshipped and gifts are offered to them. Ancient poets and philosophers have written beautiful poems and books in praise of rice. Rice is also seen as a symbol of fertility which is why in the West we used to throw rice at the bride and groom, although now this has been replaced by paper confetti.

Beautifully carved rice barns are built to please the rice spirits

Rice in the Middle East and Europe

Although wheat and potatoes are the main staple crops, Middle Eastern people and Europeans do have many delicious ways of cooking rice. In the seventh century, the Muslim conquerors known as the Moors, brought many new foods and ideas into the lands they conquered. Rice was one of these foods.

When the Moors conquered Spain they grew rice in the marshy valleys. The most famous Spanish dish is **paella**, which is similar to a **pilaff** but with meat, seafood and vegetables, saffron and tomatoes. At special Spanish festivals, huge paellas are cooked in great open pans over charcoal. From Spain, rice grains were introduced into northern Italy in the Po Valley. These rices were cooked to a creamy consistency and became known as **risotto**.

In Persia, the Moors adopted the **cuisine** of the country including many elaborate rice dishes called pilaffs or **pilavi**. When the Muslim conquerors took control of Northern India, to set up the Mogul empires, they took with them court cooks to recreate the aromatic rice dishes with spices such as saffron and cardamom, piled high with vegetables, meats, nuts and dried fruits. These then became popular in India as **pilaus**.

Paella is a famous Spanish dish made of rice

In Persia (now called Iran) the special New Year dish is *Sabsi pilau*. This is made from **basmati** rice tossed with chopped green herbs and served with golden spiced fish. The rice is cooked very slowly in an enclosed pot so a golden crust forms on the bottom, known as *tadeeg*. This is broken up and served on the rice.

In Greece and Turkey, rice – together with pine nuts, currants and dill – is wrapped in pickled vine leaves and simmered in water, olive oil and lemon juice to make *dolmades*. These are served as part of the popular *meze* course, as appetizers.

Sabsi pilau – a special Iranian rice dish

A stirring dish

Italy's most famous rice dish, **risotto**, is prepared with round grains that are very creamy. It is cooked by a special technique, adding hot stock to the rice in stages and stirring almost constantly. It is eaten with a spoon. There are many hundreds of varieties of Italian rice, grown mainly in the Po Valley. These include pudding rice used in many European desserts and for canned rice pudding.

Lovely rice puddings

Several European countries have creamy rice puddings as national favourites. Portugal has a popular rice dessert called *arroz doce*, topped with ground cinnamon.

Scandinavian countries have a similar rice dessert served at Christmas. In France, a cake of rice, cream, eggs and sugar is baked to become *gâteau au riz*, whilst Belgians enjoy rice tarts.

Rice for breakfast

Americans, Australians and Europeans eat breakfast **cereals** made with puffed rice. There is also an Indian-style brunch dish of rice, flaked smoked fish, eggs and spices called *kedgeree*. This evolved during the days of the British Raj and was inspired by a spicy dish of rice and lentils called *kitchiri*. This is a good example of a dish crossing cultural boundaries – an Indian family dish becoming a British favourite.

Rice in the New World

Long grain and easy-cook rices are popular in the southern states of the United States of America and the West Indies, especially in and around the areas where they are grown.

Rice in Louisiana

Plain boiled white rice is served with spicy *gumbos* or meat stews that include the African vegetable okra – a legacy from the slave plantations. *Jambalaya* is a dish similar to Spanish **paella** but made with a long grain rice, flavoured with chilli, peppers, spicy sausage, chicken, ham or seafood.

West Indian rice

The West Indies have a good tradition of rice cooking. Perhaps the most popular dish in most of the islands is *Rice 'n' peas*. This is a dish of white rice and dried *gunga* or pigeon peas, or red kidney beans. It is sometimes flavoured with coconut milk and dried thyme. In the days of sugar plantations, owners would feed their workers parboiled rice, which is still popular today.

Wild rice – the caviar of grains

Early American settlers learnt to use many foods from the native Americans, one of which was a grain which they called **wild rice**. In fact wild rice is not related botanically to rice at all, but is a different **species**.

Wild rice is grown in north west America and Canada, although much is now cultivated in California. It occurs naturally around lakes so people harvest it by hand from canoes. The best quality wild rice still comes from this area. When wild rice is cooking it imparts a wonderful aroma of new grass and can be used in casseroles, as well as in a traditional stuffing for turkey. Over three-quarters of all wild rice sold in the United States of America is eaten at the festival of Thanksgiving in November.

A favourite rice dish in the West Indies is called Rice 'n' peas

Wild rice grows naturally around the shores of lakes in Canada and the USA

Rice in Australia

Many Australian people like eating rice – perhaps because their country is near to Asia and they enjoy the Asian **cuisine**. All Australian rice is grown in New South Wales in the Riverina region, where there is ample water from melting snow in the Snowy Mountains for **irrigation**. Most Australian rice is short or round grain.

Australian rice farmers grow their rice in a special way, alternating rice harvests with sheep and cattle-grazing and growing other **cereal** crops over a period of five to seven years. This is called a 'rotation system'. It adds natural manures from the animals to the soil and helps defeat weeds and pests naturally. This means very few chemicals or artificial fertilizers are needed.

Rice and health

Rice is a starchy food. Nutritionists classify it as a **complex carbohydrate**. This means that it gives our bodies a lot of energy which is released into our blood slowly and so gives us good stamina.

Rice for sports

Sports performers like starchy foods such as rice because the energy from it keeps them playing well for longer. Also, the energy from complex carbohydrates can be used by the body more quickly than the energy from fats. The muscles can be refuelled more efficiently.

Rice is a healthy, high-energy food popular with athletes

What else is in rice?

Athletes also need good intakes of the B-group vitamins, which are important as they help the body to release energy from food. Rice is a good source of these vitamins. It is also very low in fat and salt, and is a good source of the minerals phosphorus, iron and zinc which are needed to keep our bodies in top condition.

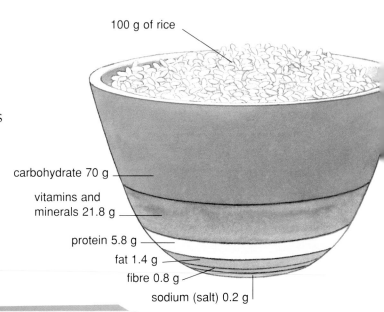

100 g of rice

carbohydrate 70 g

vitamins and minerals 21.8 g

protein 5.8 g

fat 1.4 g

fibre 0.8 g

sodium (salt) 0.2 g

Rice is a good source of vitamins and minerals

Healthy diet pyramid

If we want to be in really good health, over half our calories each day should come from starchy foods such as rice, pasta, bread and potatoes. We should aim to eat good portions each meal. A 50 g portion of rice (uncooked weight) will give you about 140 kilocalories and 36 g of carbohydrate.

To help us plan our healthy eating diet, nutritionists suggest we think of the food we eat as being like a pyramid. Starchy foods, such as rice, should be in the largest part of the pyramid at the bottom, together with fruit and vegetables, then **dairy products**, meat and fish, and right at the top, a very small amount of fat and sugar.

Rice and proteins

There is not much **protein** in rice because of the high level of **carbohydrate**. However, what there is can be digested by our bodies quickly. This rice – or vegetable – protein can also be combined with proteins from pulses such as beans, lentils or split peas (*dhal*). This makes a complete and higher amount of protein than if both foods were served separately. That is why many of the world's great rice dishes have pulses – such as peas or beans – in them. Such dishes include Indian *kitchiri* (rice and lentils) and in China and Japan – rice with tofu (a soya bean curd).

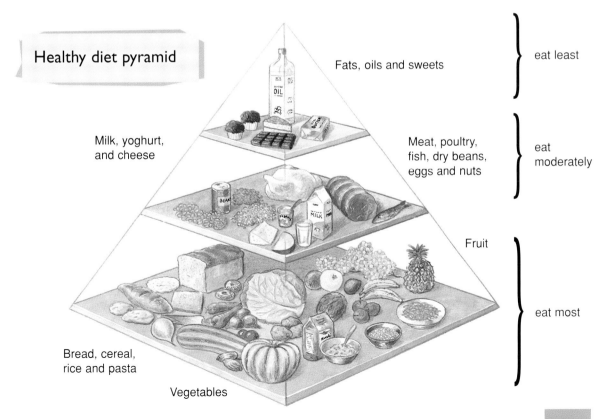

Healthy diet pyramid

Fats, oils and sweets — eat least

Milk, yoghurt, and cheese

Meat, poultry, fish, dry beans, eggs and nuts — eat moderately

Fruit

Bread, cereal, rice and pasta

Vegetables — eat most

Experiments with rice

What does rice starch look like?

To find out, you can rinse and soak uncooked rice grains in water several times and see how much starch you can wash from the surface of the grains.

You will need:

- scales
- 2 large glass bowls
- water for rinsing and soaking the rice
- about 400 g white rice

Do not use parboiled or easy-cook rice for this – basmati or long grain rice will be ideal.

What to do:

1 Measure two equal portions of rice. Put half the rice into one glass bowl.
2 Fill the bowl two-thirds full with cold water and swirl the grains with your hand. Set aside.
3 Put the remaining rice into the other bowl and also fill two-thirds full with cold water. Swirl with your hand, count to five then tip the water out, leaving the wet rice behind.
4 Fill with water again, swirl and count to five, then tip out the water. Repeat three times more (five times altogether), leaving the water in the bowl after the last time you do this.
5 Place the second bowl next to the first bowl and leave both undisturbed for 20 minutes. You should be able to see a difference. The more cloudy bowl will have a lot of starch suspended in it.

How much water is absorbed by rice in cooking?

You will need:

- scales
- measuring cup
- large saucepan
- colander
- kitchen timer
- rice
- water for boiling the rice

For best results, boil the rice in a lot of water.
Ideally use long grain rice for this, not parboiled.

What to do:

1 Fill a measuring cup (about 250 ml) to the top with uncooked rice. Weigh the rice and note the weight.
2 Bring a large pan of water to the boil. When the water boils, stir in the rice and time it from the moment the water returns to the boil. For **basmati** rice allow 10 minutes, for long grain rice allow 12 minutes, for **risotto** or short grain rices allow about 15 minutes.

3 When the rice grains are cooked and soft – but not overcooked and soggy – drain carefully in a colander. Allow the rice to sit in the colander for 5 minutes.
4 Now use the measuring cup to scoop the rice back into the scales. Note down how many cups of cooked rice the single cup of uncooked rice has produced.
5 Then note down the weight of the cooked rice. Compare both these results with the uncooked rice and you have the weight of the water absorbed and an idea of the amount by which the volume of the starch grains has increased.

Try cooking some short grain rice in the same way.
- How much water did it absorb?
- How did it compare with the long grain rice?
- Is this a good method of cooking short grain rice?

How to cook rice

There are several ways of cooking rice simply, depending on the type of grain. Here are just two. Before you start ask as adult to help you.

A bowl of perfect rice

Absorption – the covered pan method

You will need:

Ingredients

- rice
- water
- salt
- olive oil or butter (or margarine)
- chopped parsley

Equipment

- large tea cup
- medium-size saucepan with a tight-fitting lid
- kitchen timer
- metal fork
- serving platter

What to do:

1 Pour long grain rice or easy-cook (parboiled) rice into a large tea cup and smooth the top to level it. Tip the rice into a medium-size saucepan.

2 Add 2 cups of cold water and half a teaspoon salt (if you like). Bring to the boil, stirring once.

3 When the water starts to boil, cover with a tight-fitting lid and turn the heat right down. Cook for about 12 minutes without lifting the lid, or you will let out precious steam.

4 Turn off the heat, or remove from the stove. Leave the pan, still covered, to stand for 5 minutes. This helps the grains firm up a little.

5 Now lift the lid and add either 2 tablespoons olive oil or a large knob of butter or margarine. Stir it in with a metal fork. Toss in a little chopped parsley, if you like, and spoon onto a serving platter.

The open boiling method

You will need:

Ingredients

- rice
- water
- salt
- butter
- chopped parsley

Equipment

- large tea cup
- large saucepan
- kitchen timer
- large colander
- metal fork
- slotted spoon

What to do:

1 Fill a large saucepan with water, add a teaspoon or two of salt and bring to the boil.
2 Stir in one to two cups of long grain rice, depending on the size of the pan. Return the water to the boil then time from the moment it boils again.

Allow:	10 minutes for **basmati** or Thai jasmine rice
	12 minutes for long grain rice
	15–18 minutes for parboiled rices
	25 minutes for brown *basmati* rice
	40 minutes (or more) for other brown rices
	up to 50 minutes for **wild rices**

3 To see if the rice is cooked, test it by removing some grains with a slotted spoon. Cool under cold running water and press the grains between your finger and thumb. If they are cooked, they should split evenly with no hard core.
4 Drain the rice in a large colander and allow it to rest for 5 minutes before forking through with some butter and herbs (if you like).

Cooking rice in a microwave oven

Rice cooks very well in a microwave oven but as these ovens vary, check the instruction book for timings etc. You will need to use a deep-sided bowl, as the water and rice can froth up.

Cooking rice in a microwave oven

Rice pilaff

Several countries have their own **pilaff** recipes, but in all the recipes the rice is first fried in some oil (with or without onion and spices). It is then cooked in a measured amount of water, generally with the pan lid on. Before cooking ask an adult to help.

You will need:

Ingredients

- 1 onion
- 1 fat clove garlic
- 2 tablespoons sunflower oil
- 1 teaspoon mild curry powder
- 200 g *basmati* rice
- 400 ml water or vegetable stock
- $\frac{1}{2}$ teaspoon salt
- small bag frozen peas (about 120 g), thawed
- large knob of butter or margarine

Equipment

- chopping board
- chopping knife
- metal garlic press
- tea cup
- medium saucepan or frying pan with a well-fitting lid
- long-handled wooden spoon
- metal fork
- oven gloves
- wooden board
- spoon
- serving platter

What to do:

1 Cut the onion in half, then peel it and chop into small pieces. Peel the garlic clove and chop it or push through a metal garlic press.

2 Place the onion, garlic and oil into a medium saucepan and heat until they start to sizzle. Cook gently for 5 minutes, stirring occasionally, until softened.

3 Stir in the curry powder, then the rice and cook for a minute.

4 Pour in the water or stock with the salt. Bring to the boil then cover with the lid and turn the heat right down to a simmer.

5 Cook for 10 minutes. Uncover carefully (because of the steam) and stir in the peas. Cook for another 2 minutes.

6 Remove the pan from the heat using an oven glove and place on a wooden board. Do not lift the lid for 5 minutes, then stir in the knob of butter or margarine, and scrve spooned onto a serving platter.

A delicious spicy *pilaff*

Rice salad

Rice salads are best made with hot, freshly cooked rice which then cools in the dressing. That way the dressing is absorbed into the grains of rice to create the nicest flavour and texture. Serve lightly chilled, but not too cold. Before cooking ask an adult to help you.

You will need:

Ingredients

- 1 quantity of hot, cooked rice from page 24 (without oil, butter or parsley)
- 4 tablespoons ready-made French dressing or vinaigrette
- salt and freshly ground black pepper
- 3 salad onions
- 2 carrots
- $\frac{1}{4}$ cucumber (about 7–8 cm)
- small, frilly lettuce
- 6 cherry tomatoes
- $\frac{1}{2}$ punnet of salad cress

Equipment

- large mixing bowl
- chopping board
- sharp chopping knife
- grater
- large mixing spoon
- teaspoon
- serving dish

What to do:

1 Cook the plain boiled rice as in the recipe on page 24. Tip it carefully into a large mixing bowl. Mix in the dressing as the rice is cooling, as this helps to develop the flavour. Season to taste and leave to cool completely.
2 Peel and chop the salad onions, cutting them diagonally. Peel the carrots and grate them coarsely.
3 Cut the cucumber into halves, lengthways, and use a teaspoon to scrape out the seeds. Cut into quarters, lengthways. Slice thinly.
4 Toss the vegetables into the rice.
5 Wash and dry the lettuce and arrange the leaves around the outside of the serving dish. Spoon the rice salad into the middle. Halve the tomatoes and arrange them around the edge. Snip the salad cress over the top. Chill slightly before serving.

Use rice to make delicious salads

Glossary

basmati a high quality rice grown at the foothills of the Himalayas

carbohydrates nutrients that give us energy. They are mixtures of carbon, hydrogen and oxygen. Rice, potatoes, pasta and bread are complex carbohydrates which give us long-lasting energy and contain other healthy nutrients; simple carbohydrates are sugars which give us a short burst of energy but little else. Sugars can also harm your teeth

cereals grains such as wheat, corn and rice that are used for food such as bread, breakfast cereals and flours

complex carbohydrate see *carbohydrates*

congee a Chinese dish of very soft rice, often eaten for breakfast, like porridge

cuisine a style of cooking – the word *cuisine* is French and means 'kitchen'

cultivation growing of crops

dairy products milk and foods made from milk such as butter and cheese

irrigation bringing water to fields with the use of dams and ditches. This helps crops such as rice which need lots of water to grow well

paddy the rice plant and seeds before the grains are released from the husks

paddy fields areas of cultivated and irrigated land where rice plants, known as paddy, are grown

paella a Spanish dish of rice, onions, garlic, saffron (a precious spice) and tomatoes cooked in a large open pan. Sometimes chicken and seafood are added, or chick peas, or sometimes game such as wild rabbits – it depends where in Spain the *paella* is made

panicle loose, irregular type of flower-head of the rice plant

pilaff a dish of rice, onions, garlic, spices and water or stock, traditionally cooked in India and the Middle East – also called *pilavi* or *pilau*

pilau see *pilaff*

pilavi see *pilaff*

protein a nutrient used by our bodies to help our muscles grow and to repair any damaged or sick parts of the body. Proteins are made of substances called amino acids. Animal proteins from meat, fish, cheese, eggs and dairy products contain all the amino acids our bodies need.

Vegetable proteins, found in nuts, pulses, cereals etc., do not have all the amino acids but if eaten with each other become complete proteins

risotto   an Italian dish of creamy round grain rice, stirred with stock, onions, garlic, olive oil and butter, then sometimes served topped with Parmesan cheese. It can also have many other ingredients added such as chicken, peas, bacon, shellfish and even squid ink

species   a group of plants or animals that can breed with each other and reproduce. There are many species of rice and many of wheats but you cannot breed plants that are half rice, half wheat. They are separate species

spikelet   the part of the flower-head of the plant, that holds the seeds

sushi   a Japanese appetizer of cooked, soft short grain rice seasoned with vinegar, sugar and salt then wrapped in thin strips of dried seaweed enclosing strips of vegetables or fish. These are then cut in dainty rounds and eaten dipped in light, pungent sauces

terraces   raised level stretches of ground, often cut into hillsides and mountains in wide steps and cultivated as rows of long, thin fields. Many terraces in Asia were built by hand hundreds of years ago where flat land was scarce

wild rice   a variety of grain that looks similar to rice, although it is not of the same *species*

winnowing   getting rid of the husk of grains that have been rubbed off after drying. On peasant farms winnowing is often done by women tossing the grains in the wind

Further reading

Developing Skills in Home Economics. C. Connell, D. Nutter, P. Tickner, J. Ridgwell. Heinemann Educational Australia, 1991

Focus on Rice. Graham Rickard. Wayland Publishers, 1987

Rice, Beans and Pasta. Roz Denny. Martin Books, 1986

Skills in Home Economics: Food. Jenny Ridgwell. Heinemann Educational, 1990

Index

America   4, 18, 22, 23
Athletes   20

Basmati   15, 22, 23, 26
Breakfast cereal   5, 17
Brown rice   12, 13

Complex carbohydrates   20
Congee   14
Cooking rice   24–25

Emperor of Japan   15

Flooded fields   10

Gelatinization of starch   13
Gumbos   18

Healthy diet pyramid   21
Healthy eating   5

International Rice Research
    Institute (IRRI)   9
Irrigation   8, 9, 10

Jambalaya   18
Jefferson, Thomas   7

Kedgeree   17
Kitchiri   17, 21

Mechanization   11
Microwave   25
Minerals   20
Moors (Muslims)   7, 16

Nutrients in rice   13, 20

Paddy fields   8, 9, 10
Paella   16, 18
Parboiled (Easycook) rice   13,
    18, 24
Persia (Iran)   16, 17
Pilafs (pilavi)   16, 26
Pilaus   15, 16
Proteins   21

Religion   15
Rice and health   5
Rice, aroma   15
Rice, Australian   19
Rice barns   15
Rice desserts   4, 17
Rice dishes   4
Rice farmers   4
Rice grains   5, 8, 10, 11, 14
Rice 'n' peas   18
Rice noodles   5
Rice products   5
Rice, refining   12, 13
Rice spirits   15
Rice varieties   5, 10, 11
Risotto   7, 17, 23

Salads   28
Sports   20
Starch   22
Sushi   14

Terraces   8, 9

Vitamins   20

Wild rice   18